GW01339889

Name:

Address:

Tel: Cell:

Email: Birthday:

Social Networks:

Name:

Address:

Tel: Cell:

Emai: Birthday:

Social Networks:

Name:

Address:

Tel: Cell:

Email: Birthday:

Social Networks:

A

Name:

Address:

Tel: Cell:

Email: Birthday:

Social Networks:

Name:

Address:

Tel: Cell:

Emai: Birthday:

Social Networks:

Name:

Address:

Tel: Cell:

Email: Birthday:

Social Networks:

A

Name:

Address:

Tel: Cell:

Email: Birthday:

Social Networks:

Name:

Address:

Tel: Cell:

Emai: Birthday:

Social Networks:

Name:

Address:

Tel: Cell:

Email: Birthday:

Social Networks:

A

Name:

Address:

Tel: Cell:

Email: Birthday:

Social Networks:

Name:

Address:

Tel: Cell:

Emai: Birthday:

Social Networks:

Name:

Address:

Tel: Cell:

Email: Birthday:

Social Networks:

B

Name:

Address:

Tel: Cell:

Email: Birthday:

Social Networks:

Name:

Address:

Tel: Cell:

Emai: Birthday:

Social Networks:

Name:

Address:

Tel: Cell:

Email: Birthday:

Social Networks:

B

Name:

Address:

Tel: Cell:

Email: Birthday:

Social Networks:

Name:

Address:

Tel: Cell:

Emai: Birthday:

Social Networks:

Name:

Address:

Tel: Cell:

Email: Birthday:

Social Networks:

B

Name:

Address:

Tel: Cell:

Email: Birthday:

Social Networks:

Name:

Address:

Tel: Cell:

Emai: Birthday:

Social Networks:

Name:

Address:

Tel: Cell:

Email: Birthday:

Social Networks:

B

Name:

Address:

Tel: Cell:

Email: Birthday:

Social Networks:

Name:

Address:

Tel: Cell:

Emai: Birthday:

Social Networks:

Name:

Address:

Tel: Cell:

Email: Birthday:

Social Networks:

C

Name:

Address:

Tel: Cell:

Email: Birthday:

Social Networks:

Name:

Address:

Tel: Cell:

Emai: Birthday:

Social Networks:

Name:

Address:

Tel: Cell:

Email: Birthday:

Social Networks:

C

Name:

Address:

Tel: Cell:

Email: Birthday:

Social Networks:

Name:

Address:

Tel: Cell:

Emai: Birthday:

Social Networks:

Name:

Address:

Tel: Cell:

Email: Birthday:

Social Networks:

C

Name:

Address:

Tel: Cell:

Email: Birthday:

Social Networks:

Name:

Address:

Tel: Cell:

Emai: Birthday:

Social Networks:

Name:

Address:

Tel: Cell:

Email: Birthday:

Social Networks:

C

Name:

Address:

Tel: Cell:

Email: Birthday:

Social Networks:

Name:

Address:

Tel: Cell:

Emai: Birthday:

Social Networks:

Name:

Address:

Tel: Cell:

Email: Birthday:

Social Networks:

D

Name:

Address:

Tel: Cell:

Email: Birthday:

Social Networks:

Name:

Address:

Tel: Cell:

Emai: Birthday:

Social Networks:

Name:

Address:

Tel: Cell:

Email: Birthday:

Social Networks:

D

Name:

Address:

Tel: Cell:

Email: Birthday:

Social Networks:

Name:

Address:

Tel: Cell:

Emai: Birthday:

Social Networks:

Name:

Address:

Tel: Cell:

Email: Birthday:

Social Networks:

D

Name:

Address:

Tel: Cell:

Email: Birthday:

Social Networks:

Name:

Address:

Tel: Cell:

Emai: Birthday:

Social Networks:

Name:

Address:

Tel: Cell:

Email: Birthday:

Social Networks:

D

Name:

Address:

Tel: Cell:

Email: Birthday:

Social Networks:

Name:

Address:

Tel: Cell:

Emai: Birthday:

Social Networks:

Name:

Address:

Tel: Cell:

Email: Birthday:

Social Networks:

E

Name:

Address:

Tel: Cell:

Email: Birthday:

Social Networks:

Name:

Address:

Tel: Cell:

Emai: Birthday:

Social Networks:

Name:

Address:

Tel: Cell:

Email: Birthday:

Social Networks:

E

Name:

Address:

Tel: Cell:

Email: Birthday:

Social Networks:

Name:

Address:

Tel: Cell:

Emai: Birthday:

Social Networks:

Name:

Address:

Tel: Cell:

Email: Birthday:

Social Networks:

E

Name:

Address:

Tel: Cell:

Email: Birthday:

Social Networks:

Name:

Address:

Tel: Cell:

Emai: Birthday:

Social Networks:

Name:

Address:

Tel: Cell:

Email: Birthday:

Social Networks:

E

Name:

Address:

Tel: Cell:

Email: Birthday:

Social Networks:

Name:

Address:

Tel: Cell:

Emai: Birthday:

Social Networks:

Name:

Address:

Tel: Cell:

Email: Birthday:

Social Networks:

F

Name:

Address:

Tel: Cell:

Email: Birthday:

Social Networks:

Name:

Address:

Tel: Cell:

Emai: Birthday:

Social Networks:

Name:

Address:

Tel: Cell:

Email: Birthday:

Social Networks:

F

Name:

Address:

Tel: Cell:

Email: Birthday:

Social Networks:

Name:

Address:

Tel: Cell:

Emai: Birthday:

Social Networks:

Name:

Address:

Tel: Cell:

Email: Birthday:

Social Networks:

F

Name:

Address:

Tel: Cell:

Email: Birthday:

Social Networks:

Name:

Address:

Tel: Cell:

Emai: Birthday:

Social Networks:

Name:

Address:

Tel: Cell:

Email: Birthday:

Social Networks:

F

Name:

Address:

Tel: Cell:

Email: Birthday:

Social Networks:

Name:

Address:

Tel: Cell:

Emai: Birthday:

Social Networks:

Name:

Address:

Tel: Cell:

Email: Birthday:

Social Networks:

G

Name:

Address:

Tel: Cell:

Email: Birthday:

Social Networks:

Name:

Address:

Tel: Cell:

Emai: Birthday:

Social Networks:

Name:

Address:

Tel: Cell:

Email: Birthday:

Social Networks:

G

Name:

Address:

Tel: Cell:

Email: Birthday:

Social Networks:

Name:

Address:

Tel: Cell:

Emai: Birthday:

Social Networks:

Name:

Address:

Tel: Cell:

Email: Birthday:

Social Networks:

G

Name:

Address:

Tel: Cell:

Email: Birthday:

Social Networks:

Name:

Address:

Tel: Cell:

Emai: Birthday:

Social Networks:

Name:

Address:

Tel: Cell:

Email: Birthday:

Social Networks:

G

Name:

Address:

Tel: Cell:

Email: Birthday:

Social Networks:

Name:

Address:

Tel: Cell:

Emai: Birthday:

Social Networks:

Name:

Address:

Tel: Cell:

Email: Birthday:

Social Networks:

H

Name:

Address:

Tel: Cell:

Email: Birthday:

Social Networks:

Name:

Address:

Tel: Cell:

Emai: Birthday:

Social Networks:

Name:

Address:

Tel: Cell:

Email: Birthday:

Social Networks:

H

Name:

Address:

Tel: Cell:

Email: Birthday:

Social Networks:

Name:

Address:

Tel: Cell:

Emai: Birthday:

Social Networks:

Name:

Address:

Tel: Cell:

Email: Birthday:

Social Networks:

H

Name:

Address:

Tel: Cell:

Email: Birthday:

Social Networks:

Name:

Address:

Tel: Cell:

Emai: Birthday:

Social Networks:

Name:

Address:

Tel: Cell:

Email: Birthday:

Social Networks:

H

Name:

Address:

Tel:					Cell:

Email:					Birthday:

Social Networks:

Name:

Address:

Tel:					Cell:

Emai:					Birthday:

Social Networks:

Name:

Address:

Tel:					Cell:

Email:					Birthday:

Social Networks:

Name:

Address:

Tel: Cell:

Email: Birthday:

Social Networks:

Name:

Address:

Tel: Cell:

Emai: Birthday:

Social Networks:

Name:

Address:

Tel: Cell:

Email: Birthday:

Social Networks:

Name:

Address:

Tel: Cell:

Email: Birthday:

Social Networks:

Name:

Address:

Tel: Cell:

Emai: Birthday:

Social Networks:

Name:

Address:

Tel: Cell:

Email: Birthday:

Social Networks:

Name:

Address:

Tel: Cell:

Email: Birthday:

Social Networks:

Name:

Address:

Tel: Cell:

Emai: Birthday:

Social Networks:

Name:

Address:

Tel: Cell:

Email: Birthday:

Social Networks:

I

Name:

Address:

Tel: Cell:

Email: Birthday:

Social Networks:

Name:

Address:

Tel: Cell:

Emai: Birthday:

Social Networks:

Name:

Address:

Tel: Cell:

Email: Birthday:

Social Networks:

J

Name:

Address:

Tel: Cell:

Email: Birthday:

Social Networks:

Name:

Address:

Tel: Cell:

Emai: Birthday:

Social Networks:

Name:

Address:

Tel: Cell:

Email: Birthday:

Social Networks:

J

Name:

Address:

Tel: Cell:

Email: Birthday:

Social Networks:

Name:

Address:

Tel: Cell:

Emai: Birthday:

Social Networks:

Name:

Address:

Tel: Cell:

Email: Birthday:

Social Networks:

J

Name:

Address:

Tel: Cell:

Email: Birthday:

Social Networks:

Name:

Address:

Tel: Cell:

Emai: Birthday:

Social Networks:

Name:

Address:

Tel: Cell:

Email: Birthday:

Social Networks:

J

Name:

Address:

Tel: Cell:

Email: Birthday:

Social Networks:

Name:

Address:

Tel: Cell:

Emai: Birthday:

Social Networks:

Name:

Address:

Tel: Cell:

Email: Birthday:

Social Networks:

K

Name:

Address:

Tel: Cell:

Email: Birthday:

Social Networks:

Name:

Address:

Tel: Cell:

Emai: Birthday:

Social Networks:

Name:

Address:

Tel: Cell:

Email: Birthday:

Social Networks:

K

Name:

Address:

Tel: Cell:

Email: Birthday:

Social Networks:

Name:

Address:

Tel: Cell:

Emai: Birthday:

Social Networks:

Name:

Address:

Tel: Cell:

Email: Birthday:

Social Networks:

K

Name:

Address:

Tel: Cell:

Email: Birthday:

Social Networks:

Name:

Address:

Tel: Cell:

Emai: Birthday:

Social Networks:

Name:

Address:

Tel: Cell:

Email: Birthday:

Social Networks:

K

Name:

Address:

Tel: Cell:

Email: Birthday:

Social Networks:

Name:

Address:

Tel: Cell:

Emai: Birthday:

Social Networks:

Name:

Address:

Tel: Cell:

Email: Birthday:

Social Networks:

L

Name:

Address:

Tel: Cell:

Email: Birthday:

Social Networks:

Name:

Address:

Tel: Cell:

Emai: Birthday:

Social Networks:

Name:

Address:

Tel: Cell:

Email: Birthday:

Social Networks:

L

Name:

Address:

Tel: Cell:

Email: Birthday:

Social Networks:

Name:

Address:

Tel: Cell:

Emai: Birthday:

Social Networks:

Name:

Address:

Tel: Cell:

Email: Birthday:

Social Networks:

L

Name:

Address:

Tel: Cell:

Email: Birthday:

Social Networks:

Name:

Address:

Tel: Cell:

Emai: Birthday:

Social Networks:

Name:

Address:

Tel: Cell:

Email: Birthday:

Social Networks:

L

Name:

Address:

Tel: Cell:

Email: Birthday:

Social Networks:

Name:

Address:

Tel: Cell:

Emai: Birthday:

Social Networks:

Name:

Address:

Tel: Cell:

Email: Birthday:

Social Networks:

M

Name:

Address:

Tel: Cell:

Email: Birthday:

Social Networks:

Name:

Address:

Tel: Cell:

Emai: Birthday:

Social Networks:

Name:

Address:

Tel: Cell:

Email: Birthday:

Social Networks:

M

Name:

Address:

Tel: Cell:

Email: Birthday:

Social Networks:

Name:

Address:

Tel: Cell:

Emai: Birthday:

Social Networks:

Name:

Address:

Tel: Cell:

Email: Birthday:

Social Networks:

M

Name:

Address:

Tel: Cell:

Email: Birthday:

Social Networks:

Name:

Address:

Tel: Cell:

Emai: Birthday:

Social Networks:

Name:

Address:

Tel: Cell:

Email: Birthday:

Social Networks:

M

Name:

Address:

Tel: Cell:

Email: Birthday:

Social Networks:

Name:

Address:

Tel: Cell:

Emai: Birthday:

Social Networks:

Name:

Address:

Tel: Cell:

Email: Birthday:

Social Networks:

N

Name:

Address:

Tel: Cell:

Email: Birthday:

Social Networks:

Name:

Address:

Tel: Cell:

Emai: Birthday:

Social Networks:

Name:

Address:

Tel: Cell:

Email: Birthday:

Social Networks:

N

Name:

Address:

Tel: Cell:

Email: Birthday:

Social Networks:

Name:

Address:

Tel: Cell:

Emai: Birthday:

Social Networks:

Name:

Address:

Tel: Cell:

Email: Birthday:

Social Networks:

N

Name:

Address:

Tel: Cell:

Email: Birthday:

Social Networks:

Name:

Address:

Tel: Cell:

Emai: Birthday:

Social Networks:

Name:

Address:

Tel: Cell:

Email: Birthday:

Social Networks:

N

Name:

Address:

Tel: Cell:

Email: Birthday:

Social Networks:

Name:

Address:

Tel: Cell:

Emai: Birthday:

Social Networks:

Name:

Address:

Tel: Cell:

Email: Birthday:

Social Networks:

Name:

Address:

Tel: Cell:

Email: Birthday:

Social Networks:

Name:

Address:

Tel: Cell:

Emai: Birthday:

Social Networks:

Name:

Address:

Tel: Cell:

Email: Birthday:

Social Networks:

O

Name:

Address:

Tel: Cell:

Email: Birthday:

Social Networks:

Name:

Address:

Tel: Cell:

Emai: Birthday:

Social Networks:

Name:

Address:

Tel: Cell:

Email: Birthday:

Social Networks:

Name:

Address:

Tel: Cell:

Email: Birthday:

Social Networks:

Name:

Address:

Tel: Cell:

Emai: Birthday:

Social Networks:

Name:

Address:

Tel: Cell:

Email: Birthday:

Social Networks:

O

Name:

Address:

Tel: Cell:

Email: Birthday:

Social Networks:

Name:

Address:

Tel: Cell:

Emai: Birthday:

Social Networks:

Name:

Address:

Tel: Cell:

Email: Birthday:

Social Networks:

P

Name:

Address:

Tel: Cell:

Email: Birthday:

Social Networks:

Name:

Address:

Tel: Cell:

Emai: Birthday:

Social Networks:

Name:

Address:

Tel: Cell:

Email: Birthday:

Social Networks:

P

Name:

Address:

Tel: Cell:

Email: Birthday:

Social Networks:

Name:

Address:

Tel: Cell:

Emai: Birthday:

Social Networks:

Name:

Address:

Tel: Cell:

Email: Birthday:

Social Networks:

P

Name:

Address:

Tel: Cell:

Email: Birthday:

Social Networks:

Name:

Address:

Tel: Cell:

Emai: Birthday:

Social Networks:

Name:

Address:

Tel: Cell:

Email: Birthday:

Social Networks:

P

Name:

Address:

Tel: Cell:

Email: Birthday:

Social Networks:

Name:

Address:

Tel: Cell:

Emai: Birthday:

Social Networks:

Name:

Address:

Tel: Cell:

Email: Birthday:

Social Networks:

Q

Name:

Address:

Tel: Cell:

Email: Birthday:

Social Networks:

Name:

Address:

Tel: Cell:

Emai: Birthday:

Social Networks:

Name:

Address:

Tel: Cell:

Email: Birthday:

Social Networks:

Q

Name:

Address:

Tel: Cell:

Email: Birthday:

Social Networks:

Name:

Address:

Tel: Cell:

Emai: Birthday:

Social Networks:

Name:

Address:

Tel: Cell:

Email: Birthday:

Social Networks:

Q

Name:

Address:

Tel: Cell:

Email: Birthday:

Social Networks:

Name:

Address:

Tel: Cell:

Emai: Birthday:

Social Networks:

Name:

Address:

Tel: Cell:

Email: Birthday:

Social Networks:

Q

Name:

Address:

Tel: Cell:

Email: Birthday:

Social Networks:

Name:

Address:

Tel: Cell:

Emai: Birthday:

Social Networks:

Name:

Address:

Tel: Cell:

Email: Birthday:

Social Networks:

R

Name:

Address:

Tel: Cell:

Email: Birthday:

Social Networks:

Name:

Address:

Tel: Cell:

Emai: Birthday:

Social Networks:

Name:

Address:

Tel: Cell:

Email: Birthday:

Social Networks:

R

Name:

Address:

Tel: Cell:

Email: Birthday:

Social Networks:

Name:

Address:

Tel: Cell:

Emai: Birthday:

Social Networks:

Name:

Address:

Tel: Cell:

Email: Birthday:

Social Networks:

R

Name:

Address:

Tel: Cell:

Email: Birthday:

Social Networks:

Name:

Address:

Tel: Cell:

Emai: Birthday:

Social Networks:

Name:

Address:

Tel: Cell:

Email: Birthday:

Social Networks:

R

Name:

Address:

Tel: Cell:

Email: Birthday:

Social Networks:

Name:

Address:

Tel: Cell:

Emai: Birthday:

Social Networks:

Name:

Address:

Tel: Cell:

Email: Birthday:

Social Networks:

S

Name:

Address:

Tel: Cell:

Email: Birthday:

Social Networks:

Name:

Address:

Tel: Cell:

Emai: Birthday:

Social Networks:

Name:

Address:

Tel: Cell:

Email: Birthday:

Social Networks:

S

Name:

Address:

Tel: Cell:

Email: Birthday:

Social Networks:

Name:

Address:

Tel: Cell:

Emai: Birthday:

Social Networks:

Name:

Address:

Tel: Cell:

Email: Birthday:

Social Networks:

S

Name:

Address:

Tel: Cell:

Email: Birthday:

Social Networks:

Name:

Address:

Tel: Cell:

Emai: Birthday:

Social Networks:

Name:

Address:

Tel: Cell:

Email: Birthday:

Social Networks:

S

Name:

Address:

Tel: Cell:

Email: Birthday:

Social Networks:

Name:

Address:

Tel: Cell:

Emai: Birthday:

Social Networks:

Name:

Address:

Tel: Cell:

Email: Birthday:

Social Networks:

T

Name:

Address:

Tel: Cell:

Email: Birthday:

Social Networks:

Name:

Address:

Tel: Cell:

Emai: Birthday:

Social Networks:

Name:

Address:

Tel: Cell:

Email: Birthday:

Social Networks:

T

Name:

Address:

Tel: Cell:

Email: Birthday:

Social Networks:

Name:

Address:

Tel: Cell:

Emai: Birthday:

Social Networks:

Name:

Address:

Tel: Cell:

Email: Birthday:

Social Networks:

T

Name:

Address:

Tel: Cell:

Email: Birthday:

Social Networks:

Name:

Address:

Tel: Cell:

Emai: Birthday:

Social Networks:

Name:

Address:

Tel: Cell:

Email: Birthday:

Social Networks:

T

Name:

Address:

Tel: Cell:

Email: Birthday:

Social Networks:

Name:

Address:

Tel: Cell:

Emai: Birthday:

Social Networks:

Name:

Address:

Tel: Cell:

Email: Birthday:

Social Networks:

U

Name:

Address:

Tel: Cell:

Email: Birthday:

Social Networks:

Name:

Address:

Tel: Cell:

Emai: Birthday:

Social Networks:

Name:

Address:

Tel: Cell:

Email: Birthday:

Social Networks:

U

Name:

Address:

Tel: Cell:

Email: Birthday:

Social Networks:

Name:

Address:

Tel: Cell:

Emai: Birthday:

Social Networks:

Name:

Address:

Tel: Cell:

Email: Birthday:

Social Networks:

U

Name:

Address:

Tel: Cell:

Email: Birthday:

Social Networks:

Name:

Address:

Tel: Cell:

Emai: Birthday:

Social Networks:

Name:

Address:

Tel: Cell:

Email: Birthday:

Social Networks:

U

Name:

Address:

Tel: Cell:

Email: Birthday:

Social Networks:

Name:

Address:

Tel: Cell:

Emai: Birthday:

Social Networks:

Name:

Address:

Tel: Cell:

Email: Birthday:

Social Networks:

V

Name:

Address:

Tel: Cell:

Email: Birthday:

Social Networks:

Name:

Address:

Tel: Cell:

Emai: Birthday:

Social Networks:

Name:

Address:

Tel: Cell:

Email: Birthday:

Social Networks:

V

Name:

Address:

Tel: Cell:

Email: Birthday:

Social Networks:

Name:

Address:

Tel: Cell:

Emai: Birthday:

Social Networks:

Name:

Address:

Tel: Cell:

Email: Birthday:

Social Networks:

V

Name:

Address:

Tel: Cell:

Email: Birthday:

Social Networks:

Name:

Address:

Tel: Cell:

Emai: Birthday:

Social Networks:

Name:

Address:

Tel: Cell:

Email: Birthday:

Social Networks:

V

Name:

Address:

Tel: Cell:

Email: Birthday:

Social Networks:

Name:

Address:

Tel: Cell:

Emai: Birthday:

Social Networks:

Name:

Address:

Tel: Cell:

Email: Birthday:

Social Networks:

W

Name:

Address:

Tel: Cell:

Email: Birthday:

Social Networks:

Name:

Address:

Tel: Cell:

Emai: Birthday:

Social Networks:

Name:

Address:

Tel: Cell:

Email: Birthday:

Social Networks:

W

Name:

Address:

Tel: Cell:

Email: Birthday:

Social Networks:

Name:

Address:

Tel: Cell:

Emai: Birthday:

Social Networks:

Name:

Address:

Tel: Cell:

Email: Birthday:

Social Networks:

W

Name:

Address:

Tel: Cell:

Email: Birthday:

Social Networks:

Name:

Address:

Tel: Cell:

Emai: Birthday:

Social Networks:

Name:

Address:

Tel: Cell:

Email: Birthday:

Social Networks:

W

Name:

Address:

Tel: Cell:

Email: Birthday:

Social Networks:

Name:

Address:

Tel: Cell:

Emai: Birthday:

Social Networks:

Name:

Address:

Tel: Cell:

Email: Birthday:

Social Networks:

XY

Name:

Address:

Tel: Cell:

Email: Birthday:

Social Networks:

Name:

Address:

Tel: Cell:

Emai: Birthday:

Social Networks:

Name:

Address:

Tel: Cell:

Email: Birthday:

Social Networks:

XY

Name:

Address:

Tel: Cell:

Email: Birthday:

Social Networks:

Name:

Address:

Tel: Cell:

Emai: Birthday:

Social Networks:

Name:

Address:

Tel: Cell:

Email: Birthday:

Social Networks:

XY

Name:

Address:

Tel: Cell:

Email: Birthday:

Social Networks:

Name:

Address:

Tel: Cell:

Emai: Birthday:

Social Networks:

Name:

Address:

Tel: Cell:

Email: Birthday:

Social Networks:

XY

Name:

Address:

Tel: Cell:

Email: Birthday:

Social Networks:

Name:

Address:

Tel: Cell:

Emai: Birthday:

Social Networks:

Name:

Address:

Tel: Cell:

Email: Birthday:

Social Networks:

2

Name:

Address:

Tel: Cell:

Email: Birthday:

Social Networks:

Name:

Address:

Tel: Cell:

Emai: Birthday:

Social Networks:

Name:

Address:

Tel: Cell:

Email: Birthday:

Social Networks:

Z

Name:

Address:

Tel: Cell:

Email: Birthday:

Social Networks:

Name:

Address:

Tel: Cell:

Emai: Birthday:

Social Networks:

Name:

Address:

Tel: Cell:

Email: Birthday:

Social Networks:

Z

Name:

Address:

Tel: Cell:

Email: Birthday:

Social Networks:

Name:

Address:

Tel: Cell:

Emai: Birthday:

Social Networks:

Name:

Address:

Tel: Cell:

Email: Birthday:

Social Networks:

Z

Name:

Address:

Tel: Cell:

Email: Birthday:

Social Networks:

Name:

Address:

Tel: Cell:

Emai: Birthday:

Social Networks:

Name:

Address:

Tel: Cell:

Email: Birthday:

Social Networks:

Printed in Great Britain
by Amazon